T0114785

FOLLOW THE LIGHT TO CHRISTMAS

A CHRISTMAS LEGACY

Donna Murphy Perry

WESTBOW
PRESS®
A DIVISION OF THOMAS NELSON
& ZONDERVAN

WestBow Press books may be ordered through booksellers or by contacting:

WestBow Press
A Division of Thomas Nelson & Zondervan
1663 Liberty Drive
Bloomington, IN 47403
www.westbowpress.com
844-714-3454

Because of the dynamic nature of the Internet, any web addresses or
links contained in this book may have changed since publication and
may no longer be valid. The views expressed in this work are solely those
of the author and do not necessarily reflect the views of the publisher,
and the publisher hereby disclaims any responsibility for them.

Any people depicted in stock imagery provided by Getty Images are
models, and such images are being used for illustrative purposes only.
Certain stock imagery © Getty Images.

Interior Image Credit: Diane Murphy

ISBN: 979-8-3850-0967-1 (sc)
ISBN: 979-8-3850-0968-8 (hc)
ISBN: 979-8-3850-0969-5 (e)

Library of Congress Control Number: 2023919213

Print information available on the last page.

WestBow Press rev. date: 11/29/2023

To my husband, John Perry, whose steadfast heart
has been God's provision of love and protection
for me over the last fifty blessed years.
Also to our children and grandchildren who have
been God's provision of joy for my heart.
Children: John Andrew, Ashley, Emily, Brian
Grandchildren: John David, Katelyn, Caroline, Madelyn

Illustrator's Dedication
The illustrations in this book are dedicated
to my Daddy and Mama.

CONTENTS

ACKNOWLEDGMENTS

Books don't "just happen." Even though I have put the words on paper, there are many people who have been part of the process. Much of the work has turned out to be a family project. My sister, Diane Murphy, has been an artist since she was three years old. She came through with flying colors (even though all the illustrations are black and white). Using her God-given talent, she captured the essence of each devotion with wonderful simplicity.

Technology is an area in which there is ample opportunity for someone to provide assistance. My brother, Danny Murphy, has been our family's technology guru since the dawn of PCs. He has always been generous with his time, knowledge, and patience. As I have worked to publish this book, I have needed all three traits in abundance.

There are times in our lives when someone's influence is as powerful as their actions. My friend, Ann Gainey, provided the "can do" motivation I needed to get the job done. Her enthusiasm and example helped create the necessary courage for me to move forward with this project.

My children were my first editors. Their encouragement and input were invaluable. They also provided inspiration because they are the recipients of this legacy.

My husband, John, was the most important person in the process. He was always the first to hear every devotion. He cheered me on, he gave me honest input, and he was generous when cost was involved. In essence, this is our book and our legacy. He loved me through it, and I love him back.

To God be the glory for it all!

FOREWORD

The completion of this book has brought me great joy. I watched as my children, Donna, Diane, and Danny came together to create something that will, hopefully, touch the lives of others for a long time. This is also part of my legacy.

At the age of eighty-eight, I have seen a lot of Christmas celebrations and learned many important life lessons through the years. The Christmases of my childhood were different than today. Being raised in a farming community during the 1930s and 1940s meant life was much simpler. The community nativity program was a big event and children usually found one toy and an orange in their stocking. I have fond memories of lots of good food and family time. It may seem meager compared to how Christmas is celebrated today, but it taught me to be grateful and being grateful can give a person a happier perspective on life.

Another aspect I recall about being part of a small community was the fact that we relied on each other. Farming was hard manual work and accidents happened, but neighbors were there to help one another. Nothing was free, but hard times drew people together. We took Jesus's command to "love one another" very seriously.

World War II also impacted my childhood. I remember the upheaval it caused in all the families around me. Our young men were called into service and a lot a women went to work in factories. Rationing of gas, sugar, coffee, and even shoes proved necessary, but love of country and patriotism ran high. Learning to be self-sacrificing was difficult, but the hardest sacrifice to bear was the loss of life and the separation from loved ones. Praying was almost as common as breathing. We could not change the world at war, but we did a lot of praying.

Those were hard years. I have lived long enough to realize that each generation has its own unique sorrows and joys. The challenges today are very different, but the same virtues of faith, honesty, and integrity live on in the hearts of good men and women. We must continue to teach our children, grandchildren, and great-grandchildren these timeless values so they will continue to exist in the hearts of future generations.

Part of the legacy my mother left me was Psalm 30:5 KJV: "Weeping may endure for a night, but joy cometh in the morning."

Fay Melton Arendall

FOLLOW THE LIGHT TO LEGACY

There are aspects of your life that will last longer than you do. Some of your material possessions may be around for many generations. They will be called antiques. Your reputation could be a subject of conversation even after you are gone. It will be called memories. Most importantly, the sacred truths in which you believed during your lifetime will continue to be true. However, will they be recalled?

The next generation will not automatically assimilate into their lives the biblical truth you hold in your heart. If you are to have any influence on those who will come after you, you must be intentional about sharing the values, virtues, and truths that can shape their lives now and for years to come.

Follow the Light to Christmas was written with this distinct purpose in mind. It can be utilized year after year to reinforce the eternal truths expressed in the Christmas story. Strong Christmas traditions can implant firm beliefs that will outlast all of us.

This book is centered on reminding us to bring glory to God as we celebrate Christmas. What greater legacy can you pass to those you love than the recognition of God's glory revealed in His Son, Jesus!

"This will be written for the generation to come, that a people yet to be created may praise the Lord." (Psalm 102:18 NKJV)

DEVOTIONS

DECEMBER
1

GET READY!

Follow the Light to Advent

Advent refers to the arrival of something important. I have seen the word used in relation to the advent of TV, the advent of the Space Age, and the advent of computers. Many of us have experienced personal advents, such as weddings and births.

Usually, these advents require considerable preparation. Preparing for elaborate weddings can require a host of professionals and a boatload of money. The mountain of details needing attention can be overwhelming. Preparing for the birth of a child can mean much time spent on baby showers, nurseries, doctor visits, and childbirth classes.

Sometimes we run the risk of concentrating so intently on the arrangements for an important event that we neglect the need to prepare our hearts. Unfortunately, there have been times when the couple to be married has put much emphasis on the wedding, but little thought has been given to the marriage. How tragic it would be if getting ready for a baby overshadowed the joy of the child's arrival.

We face this dilemma every Christmas. No event can compare to the celebration of the Christ child, yet it is easy to get caught up in a frenzy of activities as we celebrate the season. We are susceptible to being consumed with the trappings of Christmas and totally missing the essence of Christmas.

To celebrate the advent of the Christ child this Christmas, be intentional, and take time to focus on that which magnifies and glorifies Jesus. All the things we do that make Christmastime sparkle with happiness are nice, but the most significant traditions are those that capture the true joy of the source of Christmas. This year and every year, prepare your hearts to receive the newborn King.

"Prepare the way for the Lord, make straight paths for him." (Luke 3:4B NIV)

Individual Activity: Recall some of the memorable events in your life (a new job, a dream vacation, or winning a competition). Recall the effort required to prepare for each experience. Now focus on preparing for your Christmas experience.

Family Activity: Think of an important family event that requires preparation, like birthday celebrations or vacations. What did you do to prepare for these events? Make a list of what you can do to prepare for Christmas. Remember to include Jesus!

To Do List
- put up Christmas tree
- get lights on the tree
- help children decorate tree
- buy presents on list
- pick up Maw Maw
- bake cookies
- plan Christmas menu
- start groc. list

YOUR REFLECTIONS

DECEMBER

2

HAPPY BIRTHDAY!

Follow the Light to the Guest of Honor

Most people love a good birthday celebration. At my third birthday party, I was surrounded by family and friends playing games in our front yard. Mama had made a homemade cake with candles, and everyone sang a less than perfect rendition of the "Happy Birthday" song. I was the center of attention.

Now my grandchildren have wonderful parties where every detail serves to carry out the theme selected by the birthday child. These themes have included a monster truck party, a Barbie party, and a strawberry party, to name a few. Each event is designed to honor and delight the special birthday boy or girl. It is their time to shine!

I have attended a birthday party or two when this was not the case. Have you ever witnessed a child at someone else's party who wanted to open the presents, blow out the candles, and get the first piece of cake? If so, then you know there is a time to explain to this child that it is not their party, and this is not about them.

Christmas is a birthday celebration. It is Jesus's birthday party. He loves for us to decorate our homes for His party. We are all invited to have fun playing games, eating cake, singing songs, and giving presents. He wants us to spend time with our friends and family on His special day. However, may we never be like the child who wants to steal the show at someone else's party. May we realize it is not about us. Make this Christmas season a time when Jesus is the center of everyone's adoration. Make Him the guest of honor at all your celebrations, and remember to say, "Happy birthday, Jesus!"

"For there is born to you this day in the city of David a Savior, who is Christ the Lord." (Luke 2:11 NKJV)

Individual Activity: Contemplate what it means to live a life more concerned about others than yourself. Think of someone you know who embodies this principle.

Family Activity: Christmas is the time of year when we want to show Jesus that we love Him. As a family, sing "Happy Birthday" to Jesus!

YOUR REFLECTIONS

DECEMBER
3

MERRY CHRISTMAS

Follow the Light to the Laughter

Some of the merriest moments of our lives happen while we celebrate our Christmas traditions: attending Christmas parties, decorating Christmas trees, visiting Santa, hanging stockings, baking cookies, wrapping presents, exchanging gifts, singing Christmas songs, watching Christmas specials on TV, feasting on holiday food, receiving Christmas cards, and the list goes on.

You could conclude that all this is secular in nature and runs the risk of missing the true meaning of Christmas. This would be true, unless the foundation of your Christmas fun is faith. Your laughter and merriment can bring joy to God's heart. God gave His people, Israel, many festivals to observe. Some observances were solemn occasions and others were meant to be celebrations of joy! The Hebrew word for *celebrate* can be translated as "to be giddy." This would be the perfect word to describe old Scrooge when he woke up on Christmas morning after an eventful night.

God created us with a huge capacity for happiness and the ability to enjoy life. At times, Jesus must have been a fun person, or the children would not have wanted to be with Him. Just as you delight in the laughter of a dearly loved child when they open a gift from you, our heavenly Father delights in our happiness when we open our hearts to His gift of grace.

Invite Jesus to be a part of all your festivities this Christmas and thank Him for all the fun. May the "merry" in your Christmas come from your love of celebrating Jesus.

"Let the righteous be glad; let them rejoice before God; yes, let them rejoice exceedingly." (Psalm 68:3 NKJV)

Individual Activity: Get comfortable and watch a funny Christmas movie.

Family Activity: Tell funny jokes, make silly faces, or tickle each other. Make one another laugh. Remind yourselves that God gave us the ability to laugh, and He loves when His children are happy, especially at Christmas!

YOUR REFLECTIONS

DECEMBER

4

CHRISTMAS FEAST

Follow the Light to the Banquet

Christmas can be a delight for all our senses, especially taste. We all have witnessed the gathering of the Whos down in Whoville when they eat their roast beast or watched as a repentant Ebenezer Scrooge orders the biggest turkey in town for the Cratchits' Christmas feast or drooled as we viewed countless holiday TV commercials featuring a family assembled around a table loaded with culinary delights.

In our family, feasting is, and always has been, a significant part of every celebration. Any event worth commemorating involves an array of dishes prepared by people whose skills were honed by the cumulative experiences of previous generations of excellent cooks. Food has the power to awaken remembrances of the past and the ability to comfort us in the present. When eating delicious food, the enjoyment I experience in my mouth connects to a place in my heart where pleasant memories reside.

This enjoyment we physically feel when we feast on food, we can also experience spiritually when we feast on the things of God.

"Taste and see that the Lord is good; blessed is the one who takes refuge in him." (Psalm 34:8 NIV)

Christmas can be a spiritual feast. We can fill our souls with His presence just as we fill our stomachs with food. When we focus on Jesus at Christmas, we take Him into our hearts, and He becomes our spiritual nourishment. He is the Bread of Life and has prepared a banquet table for us. May we all feast on the goodness of God this Christmas.

"Then Jesus declared, "I am the bread of life. Whoever comes to me will never go hungry, and whoever believes in me will never be thirsty." (John 6:35 NIV)

Individual Activity: Satisfy the hunger in your heart with the words of Jesus. Read John 6:35 aloud.

Family Activity: Take a slice of bread and divide it into pieces for each person. Read John 6:35 aloud. Say a short prayer of thanksgiving for Jesus and then eat the bread!

YOUR REFLECTIONS

DECEMBER

5

CHRISTMASTIME

Follow the Light to Time Everlasting

"It's that time of year when the world falls in love
Every song you hear seems to say, 'Merry Christmas.'"

"The Christmas Waltz" reminds us of the special time surrounding Christmas. The holidays are an interlude in our lives when we direct our focus on more than the daily grind. We mark our calendars as we look forward to this special day.

The evergreen wreaths on our doors at Christmas symbolize this idea of time. The circle with no end represents the truth of everlasting life, the purpose of the first Christmas. *Everlasting* refers to an existence that has a beginning but has no end. This concept is difficult for our finite minds to fully comprehend. Even more overwhelming is the thought of *eternal*, which is being with no beginning and no end. Only God is the eternal, "was, is, and is to come."

As humans on this earth, we are acutely aware that we are bound by time. We were not in control of when our time started, we cannot prevent time from passing, and we do not know when our time on earth will end. However, we have been given the opportunity to use our time here to shape our everlasting.

The Bible teaches us the things we do to honor the Christ of Christmas will last forever. Christmas is the perfect season to spend time investing in our everlasting. The experiences of the here and now demand our attention be directed to that which is temporary. However, even the transient can be infused with unending meaning when our heart motivation is to bring glory to God. Oh, that Christmastime would reside in our hearts every day and always.

"Praise be to the Lord, the God of Israel, from everlasting to everlasting. Then all the people said 'Amen' and 'Praise the Lord.'" (1 Chronicles 16:36 NIV)

Individual Activity: Look at a clock with a second hand to remind yourself how quickly time flies. Ask yourself how much time do I spend on things that are everlasting.

Family Activity: Show everyone a picture of a straight line and a circle. Point out the beginning and end of the straight line. Now examine the circle and explain that it really has no beginning and no ending. God is like the circle.

YOUR REFLECTIONS

DECEMBER

6

WHAT HE LEFT BEHIND

Follow the Light to Love

Mother Teresa exemplified a life of sacrificial love. She strongly believed that a life not lived for others is not a life.

She was born in what is now North Macedonia to a financially comfortable family. At the age of eighteen, she left home to join the sisters of Loreto in Ireland, never to see her family again. One year later, she transferred to India where she took her vows.

In India, she taught at a high school for daughters of wealthy residents of Calcutta. After 15 years of teaching, the abject poverty that she witnesses in the city grips her heart; so, she left the convent to serve the poor. Without financial means or committed support, she moved to a hovel in the slums to live amidst the victims of leprosy, the ragged, orphans begging for sustenance, and those dying alone with no one who cared.

Her love was evident, not only in what she was doing; but, also in what she was willing to give up to do it. Leaving behind family, friends, comfort, security, safety, and pleasant surroundings proved the authenticity of her love.

Even so, this does not compare to the depth of sacrifice Jesus made when he clothed himself in humanity. He left heaven, a place where "no eye has seen, nor ear heard, neither has it entered into the heart of man" the wonder of it all. Not only did He willingly leave this wonderful place, He also left behind His honor and glory. Most excruciating of all, He gave up His heavenly holiness and became sin for us, causing Him to be forsaken on the cross by His Father who was in heaven.

This Christmas may we fully grasp the extent of the sacrifice Jesus made to make a way for us to become His children. His great love for us is proven by what He was willing to leave behind when He became the baby in the manger.

"He is despised and rejected of men, a Man of sorrows and acquainted with grief, and we hid as it were our faces from Him. He was despised, and we esteemed Him not." (Isaiah 53:3 NIV)

Individual Activity: Answer the question, "What am I willing to give up to honor Christ this Christmas?"

Family Activity: Ask everyone if they would share one of their possessions with you. Then request that they give you all their possessions. Was anyone willing to give up all their possessions? Jesus was willing to give up everything to be our Savior!

YOUR REFLECTIONS

DECEMBER

7

THE INCARNATION

Follow the Light to Immanuel
(God with Us)

When I turn back the pages of time in my mind, I vividly recall one small incident that has pleasantly lingered in my memory for over fifty years. On a Christmas morning when I was a young girl, I ripped off the paper of one of my gifts. It was a cowgirl tea set and I thought it was the best tea set ever. I was so enamored with my new dishes that my Daddy decided we should serve our breakfast on them. I can still remember the joy of sitting at my little kid's table (the one Daddy had built for me) and watching Mama dip scrambled eggs onto our miniature plates. Daddy looked so funny sitting on the little kid bench eating from the small plate with his knees nearly hitting his chin. For that moment in time, he entered my little girl world, and I knew him in a different way. Daddy did not stop being my Daddy when he ate with me. He simply became Daddy in a way I could know him better.

This simple tale is an expression of a profound and mysterious truth, the incarnation of Christ.

"The great miracle of incarnation slips into the ordinary life of a child." Oswald Chambers.

"And the Word became flesh, and dwelt among us, and we beheld His glory, the glory as of the only begotten of the Father, full of grace and truth." (John 1:14 NKJV)

Jesus entered Earth's space and time to accomplish the Father's plan of salvation for us. He experienced life on earth as we do. When He entered our reality. He did not cease to be God, but He became God in a way we could know him better. We rejoice that He became like us, so we could someday be with Him forever.

"I keep asking that the God of our Lord Jesus Christ, the glorious Father, may give you the Spirit of wisdom and revelation, so that you may know him better." (Ephesians 1:17 NIV)

Individual Activity: Reflect on ways you can get to know God better in this season of Christmas.

Family Activity: Tell your child what Christmas meant to you when you were young. For a moment, become a child so that your child can know you better.

YOUR REFLECTIONS

DECEMBER

8

THE BEST THING ABOUT CHRISTMAS

Follow the Light to the Gift

If you ask young children, "What is the best thing about Christmas?" practically all of them will say, "Presents." This is simply another way of saying "I will get toys." When I was a kid, I shared that sentiment. I would pour over the Sears catalog for weeks prior to Christmas imagining the fun I would have if I got the toys I wanted. Many times, I did get exactly what I asked for, and I would be ecstatic. While reminiscing about those happy moments, I realize all those gifts are now long gone.

Jesus also received presents when He was a small boy. The Magi wanted to find Him so badly, they traveled many miles to a town called Bethlehem. They brought him valuable gifts that would later enable his family to protect his life. I am sure, even as a young child, Jesus enjoyed the shiny gold, the sweet-smelling perfume, and the nice men who came to see him. Even so, those presents are now long gone also.

However, the wise men were wise because, somehow, they realized the little boy to whom they were giving gold, frankincense, and myrrh, was the most important gift of all. We now understand, even better than the Wise Men, the significance of the offering God gave us when He gave us His son. He is the King of a kingdom that will never pass away and the gift of Himself to us will be the only present we will ever receive that will last forever. The children are right, the best thing about Christmas is the gift.

"Thanks be to God for his indescribable gift!" (2 Corinthians 9:15 NKJV)

Individual Activity: As you purchase presents this Christmas, stop, and compare each gift with the value of God's "indescribable gift."

Family Activity: Look at toys in a catalogue or online. Let everyone pick out something they would like to have. Ask if any of these items will last forever. Emphasize that Jesus is the only everlasting gift.

YOUR REFLECTIONS

DECEMBER
9

BITTERSWEET GIVING

Follow the Light to Blessing

Once I saw a TV program that featured research involving three separate children around the age of ten who were the son or daughter of three different single mothers. Individually, each child was given a very desirable toy. After expressing their delight with the gift, each one was offered a lovely piece of jewelry which they could give to their mom. All eagerly accepted the gift for their mother also.

Then, they were informed they could only have one of the two gifts. You could see the inner struggle on each child's face, one to the point of tears. Even so, every child chose the gift for their mother, rather than keeping their toy. When each mother was told of the sacrifice her child had made for her, they were overwhelmed with bittersweet emotion and so were the children. These children knew how to give sacrificially, because they had seen it in the examples of their mothers. They had witnessed the unselfishness of their mothers' love every day.

As Christians, we know about this kind of love. We have experienced the sacrificial giving of Christ. His suffering on the cross is visual evidence of the depth of His willingness to surrender His rights to attain our salvation.

May His example move us to exhibit selfless love to others. May we commit acts of love that do not demand credit or have any strings attached. If you are the recipient of bittersweet giving this Christmas, you are blessed. If you are the giver, you are blessed most of all; because, receiving love can make you happy, but giving love can bring you joy.

"Therefore, be imitators of God as dear children. And walk in love, as Christ also has loved us and given Himself for us, an offering and a sacrifice to God ..." (Ephesians 5:1,2 NKJV)

Individual Activity: This Christmas season give sacrificially to someone else. It may cost you time, money, and/or effort. Consider how the act of giving impacted you.

Family Activity: Name some unselfish acts people in your family do for each other. As a family, plan to do something thoughtful for someone else this Christmas season.

YOUR REFLECTIONS

THE CHILD WHO BROKE CHRISTMAS

Follow the Light to Mercy

It was me. I was the child who broke Christmas. The incident occurred during my sixth Christmas as I was playing around our family's Christmas tree. It was a cedar, fresh cut from the woods behind our house. Draped with shining decorations, including numerous breakable Christmas balls, this tree was the centerpiece of Christmas in our home. At least, it was until I made one false move and brought the whole thing crashing down.

Horrified by the destruction around me, I began crying loudly. My mother came running to see me surrounded by shards of glass and electric light cords. Immediately, she scooped me up to ensure I was not injured. She soon realized I was not hurt physically; but my heart was broken. Our family's Christmas was ruined, and it was my fault. The guilt of knowing I was somewhere I should not have been, doing something I should not have been doing felt awful. The fact that it also caused other people to be unhappy increased my distress.

However, instead of receiving the well-deserved reprimand and punishment, Mama dried my tears and calmed my fears. She rescued me from the shattered glass and put me in a safe place. Then, she lifted the tree to an upright position and salvaged all the decorations she could. Surprisingly, when she finished cleaning up my mess, the tree was restored to its original glory (minus a few Christmas balls). Mercy is a beautiful thing.

God's mercy is the most astounding aspect of His holy nature, and we are utterly dependent on it, just as a child in the womb of its mother. It is the motivation for Christmas. It is the impetus that drives Christ to leave heaven and become a baby in a manger. Even though we all have rebelled against His loving kindness, ignored

His grace, and, at times, even rejected Him, He continually offers us forgiveness and restoration. A broken and repentant heart is and, always will be, safe in the mercy of God. May the Holy Spirit instill this truth in your spirit this Christmas.

"Surely goodness and mercy shall follow me all the days of my life; and I will dwell in the house of the Lord forever." (Psalm 23:6 NKJV)

Individual Activity: Meditate on how important God's mercy is to you. Imagine your life without the healing hope it brings.

Family Activity: Ask if anyone has ever broken something that belonged to someone else. If so, how did it make them feel? Did you want to be punished or forgiven? If you were shown mercy, were you grateful?

YOUR REFLECTIONS

DECEMBER

11

FOLLOW IN THEIR FOOTSTEPS

Follow the Light to Humility

Jesus' birth announcement is a heavenly beam that serves as a lighthouse for a group of expectant watchmen. They are the Magi, distinguished men from the East renowned for their knowledge and wisdom. Even though they are not Jewish, these learned men have studied the ancient prophecies of the Old Testament and recognize the significance of the unusual light in the night sky when it appears.

The sight of the star ignites a compelling desire to seek the source of this miraculous event. So, the journey begins. With animals loaded with necessities and treasure, they move westward headed to Jerusalem. They know who they are seeking. Finding the newborn King of the Jews is their quest.

Upon their arrival, these important officials are escorted into the presence of King Herod where they disclose the purpose of their visit. "Where is He who has been born King of the Jews?" In response, Herod calls together his own "wise men" who say the prophesied king is to be born in Bethlehem of Judea.

As the Magi head to Bethlehem about six miles south of Jerusalem, they again see the light they had seen in their homeland. The hearts of the Magi are filled with exceedingly great joy at the sight. This miraculous radiance is guiding them directly to the house where the young child lives. Upon entering the home, these influential scholars fall on their knees and worship Him.

What great faith it takes for these powerful people to look upon this small child and deem Him worthy of their worship! The most amazing thing about the Magi is not their wisdom, wealth, or power; it is their humility. May our Christmas celebrations follow in the footsteps of the Magi. Seek the Lord this Christmas and you will find Him. When you do, humble yourselves before Him and experience the joy of worship.

"Who is wise and understanding among you? Let them show it by their good life, by deeds done in the humility that comes from wisdom." (James 3:13 NIV)

Individual Activity: It takes maturity to be genuinely humble. From God's perspective, it is not a weakness; it is a sign of wisdom. Privately kneel before Him and acknowledge God's greatness.

Family Activity: Read the words of Rick Warren, "Humility is not thinking less of yourself; it is thinking of yourself less." Kneel and pray together that God would help us all be humbler.

YOUR REFLECTIONS

DECEMBER
12

TAKE A CLOSER LOOK

Follow the Light to Magnify

Through the ages, there have been all kinds of conjectures about the light in the sky seen by the Magi during the first Christmas. Could it have been a planet, or a comet or a new star? Maybe, it was not any of those things. Maybe, it was a manifestation of the shining glory of God.

If only the Magi could have observed the shining light through a telescope, we might have been given more details. Unfortunately, to our knowledge, this star-gazing instrument was not invented until 1608 AD by a Dutch eyeglass maker named Hans Lippershey. So far as we know, Galileo was the first to use it to observe celestial objects and record his observations. This exciting invention enabled people to magnify the tiny pinpoints of light in the sky and begin to understand they were not tiny lights at all, but were immense heavenly bodies.

We will never definitively know what the Magi saw, but of this I am certain: The real "star" of the Christmas nativity is Jesus. The Bible tells us in Psalm 34:3 KJV to serve as a telescope for the "star" of Christmas. "Oh, *magnify* the Lord with me, and let us exalt His name together." This verse exhorts us to declare the glory of our God, so others can get a closer look and begin to realize the magnitude of His greatness. John Piper once stated, "I will make a big God begin to look as big as he really is."

For some, God seems far away or even non-existent. He may appear distant and unimportant when compared to the people and circumstances facing them each day. Life on this earth can loom all encompassing. May our celebration of Christmas exalt Him so all may gaze through the lens of our magnification and see His glory more clearly.

"And Mary said, 'My soul magnifies the Lord, and my spirit has rejoiced in God my Savior.'" (Luke 1: 46, 47 NKJV)

Individual Activity: Choose one way you can magnify Jesus today and help someone you know see Him more clearly through your actions.

Family Activity: Go outside and pick out a large object in the sky, i.e., a star, a planet, or the moon. If available, view the object through a telescope or binoculars. If these are not available, find magnified pictures of the object on the internet. Talk about how much larger and clearer the object is when it is magnified. The same is true about Jesus. When we magnify Jesus with our actions, who He truly is becomes larger and clearer to people around us.

YOUR REFLECTIONS

DECEMBER
13

THE THREE WISE WOMEN

Follow the Light to Godly Wisdom

Mary of Nazareth in Galilee was looking forward to her upcoming wedding when she received life-changing news delivered by the angel Gabriel. The angel conveyed an astounding promise. Even though a virgin, Mary will conceive and have a baby, who will be the Son of God. As the promise unfolded, she witnessed the miracle pregnancy of Elizabeth, the reassuring dream of Joseph, the arduous journey to Bethlehem, the birth of her child, and the visit of the shepherds declaring the message of a heavenly host. This is a lot to process, so Mary kept all these things and pondered them in her heart. She pondered the work of God. The godly wisdom of this courageous woman allowed her to look at her baby and see God.

Elizabeth lived in the hill country of Judea. She, along with her husband Zacharias, descended from the priestly lineage of Aaron, the brother of Moses. Although, they lived blameless before God they were childless and well advanced in years until the angel Gabriel declared that barren Elizabeth would have a child. In the sixth month of her miraculous pregnancy, Elizabeth, Mary's kinswoman, was filled with the Holy Spirit and became the first recorded human on earth to profess Jesus as Lord. The godly wisdom of this faithful woman prompted her to affirm her faith in Jesus even when He was an unborn baby.

Anna was widowed after only seven years of marriage. She resided in the Temple where she served God with prayer and fasting night and day. It was no accident this eighty-four-year-old woman was present the day baby Jesus was brought to the Temple to be presented to God, as was the custom. The instant she saw Him, Anna recognized the significance of this child, and she gave thanks to God for sending his salvation. The godly wisdom of this grateful woman compelled her to proclaim the good news of redemption to all who would listen.

May we allow these three wise women to influence our celebration of Christmas. First, ponder the things of God deeply and often; secondly profess Jesus as Lord; and lastly, proclaim His salvation to others.

"If any of you lacks wisdom, you should ask God, who gives generously to all without finding fault, and it will be given to you." (James 1:5 NIV)

Individual Activity: Contrast wisdom and knowledge. Knowledge empowers us by revealing our choices. Then wisdom uses knowledge to make good decisions. Recall some wise decisions you have made recently.

Family Activity: Give the family examples of wise vs. unwise decisions. Ask which decision is wise and discuss why. Examples: Eat healthy food or don't eat healthy food; read the Bible or don't read the Bible; pray or don't pray.

YOUR REFLECTIONS

DECEMBER

14

LET IT BE TO ME ACCORDING TO YOUR WORD

Follow the Light to Trust

As is usually the case when angels appear to people, before their proclamation can be received they must calm the fears of the person to whom they are speaking. So, it was with Mary. At first, she was troubled when an angel appeared to her because she did not trust her visitor. Then he quieted her fear and shared the plan God had for her. She was to be the mother of the Son of God. When her fear transformed into faith, she proclaimed her trust in God, "Let it be to me according to your word." She soon expressed her feeling in a song, "My spirit has rejoiced in God my Savior."

Fear, trust, joy.

Joseph heard the news that his fiancé was with child. Since Joseph was a kind man and cared deeply for Mary, his first response was to protect her and spare her from as much pain as he could. Due to the circumstances, Joseph was troubled and afraid. As he struggled with how to handle the situation, an angel appeared to him in a dream. Of course, the angel's first words were "Do not be afraid." Then, the angel conveyed the same plan to Joseph as he had explained to Mary. Trusting the words of God, Joseph experienced the joy of marrying the woman he loved.

Fear, trust, joy.

Have you ever been through this same cycle? Have you ever held back from fully trusting Jesus because you were afraid of what he might expect you to do? We do not give trust lightly, not even to Jesus. We must believe He is trustworthy and genuinely loves us in every circumstance of our lives. Therefore, His intentions for us are not to be feared. This realization will allow us to experience the joy of release.

Mary and Joseph had vastly different plans for their lives the day before the angel appeared to Mary. Both had to make momentous decisions to trust God and let go of those plans. When they did, the decisions which may have appeared to be great sacrifices became the sources of astounding joy for them and generations to follow.

"Tis so sweet to trust in Jesus ... O for grace to trust Him more." (Hymn "Tis So Sweet to Trust in Jesus")

Individual Activity: Consider an act of faith to which you should commit. Now pray and release this act to the Lord and trust Him with the outcome.

Family Activity: Remember the first time you jumped into a swimming pool. At first, you were probably afraid. Then you saw your parent ready to catch you; so, you jumped. When you came up for air, you were thrilled. Fear, trust, joy.

YOUR REFLECTIONS

DECEMBER

15

JOSEPH'S ASSIGNMENT

Follow the Light to Grace

Joseph was a just man who found himself in a profound dilemma. When faced with the news of Mary's pregnancy, his life-long desire to follow the law created an intense conflict with his tender love for Mary. How could he be faithful to the law of God and still protect the woman he loves? God alleviated his quandary by revealing to him that the conception of Mary's baby was a work of the Holy Spirit. The holiness of Jesus was the resolution of Joseph's situation. As a result, Joseph obediently bestowed grace and married Mary.

Grace is a cherished word for Christians. "For by grace we are saved ...." But what does it mean? The literal meaning of the Hebrew word for grace involves a wall to protect life or to establish a camp for protection. Every time we see Joseph in the Christmas story, God is instructing him to protect Mary and Jesus. Joseph was God's instrument of grace (protection) for his family.

God also has a paradoxical situation like Joseph's. As a just God, how can he be true to his holy nature and still have a relationship with a broken and rebellious people? Again, Jesus is the solution, because He takes the punishment for sin and offers grace (protection) to a broken world. His sinless life, sacrificial death, and miraculous resurrection reconcile God's justice and God's mercy.

"The wisdom of God ordained a way for the love of God to deliver us from the wrath of God without compromising the justice of God." John Piper.

He is God's instrument of grace (protection) for all who would trust Him for salvation. We only require protection when we face a threat we cannot control. Christ came to offer a haven for the eternity that he knows we could not handle on our own. We need Him. May you and all those you love trust in the grace (protection) of God this Christmas.

"Marvelous, infinite, matchless grace, freely bestowed on all who believe!" (Hymn "Grace Greater than Our Sin")

Individual Activity: Think about what God's grace means to you. Is it your safe place?

Family Activity: Discuss how your house keeps you safe. Jesus is like our home. For those who choose to accept His plan, His grace will provide a safe place for their souls.

YOUR REFLECTIONS

DECEMBER

16

HEROD'S KINGDOM

Follow the Light Out of the Shadows

The king of the Jews, Herod the Great, was troubled. He was seventy years old and dying of a putrid disease; yet this was not his main concern. He was obsessed with the report of wise men from the east seeking a child born "King of the Jews," It was not a surprise that Herod pursued this child so that he might destroy him. After all, he has spent his adult years using whatever means necessary to defend his throne. He left a trail of carnage in his own family: his father-in-law, several of his ten wives, and two of his sons. In the throes of dying, he futilely sought to maintain control of the kingdom he had built.

He was not born to royalty. Herod clawed his way up the Roman Empire ladder, using whatever means necessary to acquire his kingdom. In 37 BC, the Roman Senate bestowed upon him the title of King of the Jews. This ruthless man was successful in starting his own dynasty and to his dying day he strived to keep it.

Herod's life was tragically futile. He chased all this world had to offer until his last breath, no matter what the cost. Then he died in the shadow of the only one who can give his life meaning. If only the words he said to the Magi had been sincere.

"Go and search carefully for the young Child, and when you have found Him, bring back word to me that I may come and worship Him also." Matthew 2:8 NKJV

We all strive to build our own little "kingdoms." We allow ourselves to be caught up in our personal pursuits at the expense of our relationship with God. Even though we may never be merciless like Herod, our lives can be just as pointless if all our energy is spent satisfying our own aspirations with no desire to please God.

Author C.S. Lewis describes a place he calls the Shadowlands as a place in shadow; the Son shines somewhere else, but not here. May we not dwell in the shadow as Herod did. Let this Christmas be the time you shift your focus to the light, peace, joy, and love Christ brings to those who live to honor Him.

"What good will it be for someone to gain the whole world, yet forfeit their soul? Or what can anyone give in exchange for their soul?" (Matthew 16:26 NIV)

Individual Activity: Consider how you spend your time, money, and energy. Are you living your life in the Shadowlands, or are you walking in the light of Christ?

Family Activity: Turn out the lights. Using a flashlight, make shadow figures on the wall. Talk about how the shadow figures are not real. Then turn on the Christmas tree lights. Christmas is real because Jesus is the true light of the world!

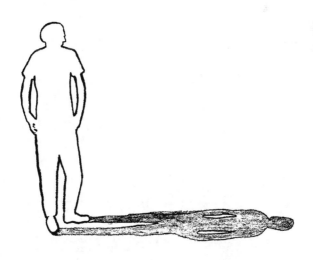

YOUR REFLECTIONS

DECEMBER

17

LOOK INSIDE THE MANGER

Follow the Light to Your Treasure

Whenever people hear the Christmas story, it is possible they identify with one character of the narrative more than another. If you are a mother, it be could Mary; if you are a husband, it could be Joseph; if you are fearful, it could be the shepherds; if you ever feel unable to help, it could be the innkeeper. Oddly enough, for me, it could be the manger. Even though an inanimate object, the manger played a significant role in the Nativity event.

Prior to the birth of Jesus, the manger was a simple feeding trough containing hay for the animals of the stable. However, the moment Mary lay the Baby in the lowly manger, its sole purpose became holding the Christ child. The angels even instructed the shepherds to identify the child by looking for the "babe lying in a manger." They then rushed to Bethlehem and found the baby lying in a manger.

When you become a Christian, your heart becomes a manger. You hold Jesus in your heart and people can identify Him when your life reflects what is in your heart.

"But we have this treasure in jars of clay to show that this all-surpassing power is from God and not from us." (2 Corinthians 4:7 NIV)

May this season be an opportunity to reflect upon the treasure we carry in our hearts. If someone looked inside your "manger" this Christmas, would they see the Savior? If your treasure is Jesus, does He have to compete with the things of this world, or does He shine brightly for others to see?

"For where your treasure is, there your heart will be also." (Luke 12:34 NIV)

Individual Activity: Think about all the things you treasure in your heart. Does your list include the Savior?

Family Activity: Place a valuable object in your child's hands. Explain to your child why they should hold the "treasure" carefully. So, it is with Jesus. We should always understand how valuable He is and live in a way that honors Him.

YOUR REFLECTIONS

DECEMBER

18

THE WARMTH OF CHRISTMAS

Follow the Light to Assurance

The Babe is covered in swaddling clothes
To protect Him from the cold.
His mother tightly wraps Him
In the blanket for her to hold.

Safe and snug, the child lies sleeping
In the manger filled with hay,
His little body resting from
The demands of Christmas Day.

The warmth of His covers
Keeps Him quiet and content,
As His parents watch lovingly
Pondering what all this meant.

The prophecy of Immanuel
has finally come to pass.
This child is "God with us."
Salvation has come at last.

His amazing love and sacrifice
Would cover all our sin,
Just as his swaddling clothes
Had once covered Him.

The warmth of this assurance
Can encompass everyone
Who will trust in the salvation
of God's only begotten Son.

"For God so loved the world that He gave His only begotten Son, that whoever believes in Him should not perish but have everlasting life." (John 3:16 NKJV)

Individual Activity: Get comfortable with a blanket and cup of hot chocolate. Remind yourself of the warm assurance you have when you place your faith in Jesus.

Family Activity: Wrap up in a cozy, warm blanket. Does it help you feel safe and secure? Knowing that Jesus came to earth to "wrap" us in His love if we trust Him should make us feel safe and secure in God's love.

YOUR REFLECTIONS

DECEMBER

19

WHAT WOULD CHRISTMAS BE WITHOUT MUSIC

Follow the Light to Worship

Envision a Christmas without music. There would be no tunes to express the cheerfulness of the season; no songs to add to the words of the Christmas story; no melodies and harmonies to lighten our hearts with sweet memories of Christmas's past. It is difficult to imagine because music is to hearing what color is to sight. No music at Christmas would be like looking at a picture of a beautiful rainbow in black, white, and shades of gray.

God has wired our brains to translate certain sound waves into music. An otolaryngologist-researcher wrote, "Music is structural, mathematical, and architectural. It is based on relationships between one note and the next. Your brain must do a lot of computing to make sense of it."

We know that our brain sometimes uses the marriage of melodies, harmonies, and words to produce deepened feelings and emotions. Sad music can make us cry; happy music can make us dance; powerful music can make us brave; but the purest music of all can make us worship.

Music elevates, heightens, and intensifies our response to God's glory. It is His gift to us, because He knows that mere words can never adequately convey our adoration of Him. It is the God-given language of worship on earth and in heaven, as proven by the heavenly host of angels who sang for the shepherds.

This holiday season let music take your celebration of Christmas to a new level. May it increase your joy and express your worship to "God in the Highest." There is nothing like a beautiful rendition of the "Hallelujah Chorus" to help you experience a little of heaven on earth.

"May they sing of the ways of the Lord, for the glory of the Lord is great." (Psalm 138:5 NIV)

Individual Activity: Sing your favorite praise chorus or hymn for an audience of one.

Family Activity: Play a rendition of the Hallelujah chorus and have everyone stand in honor of the King of King and Lord of Lords.

YOUR REFLECTIONS

DECEMBER
20

THE GREATEST DECLARATION OF ALL TIME

Follow the Light to Glory

The Magna Carta, the Declaration of Independence, the Emancipation Proclamation. Each of these famous documents proclaim the ideals of freedom for all individuals. They stand out in history as milestones lighting the way for liberty. These lofty principles are great declarations of a goal for which we should strive to obtain for all humanity.

Even though these documents express a noble quest, their message is far exceeded by the declaration of Christmas as stated by the angels who appeared to the shepherds.

"Glory to God in the highest."

Christmas represents the birth of redemption for all creation. Christ came to earth to overcome sin and death. His resurrection constructed the bridge needed to reconcile us to God. Bible commentator Matthew Henry puts it this way, "Other works of God are for His glory; but the redemption of the world is for His glory in the highest."

In other words, in the eyes of God, His plan of salvation is the ultimate, the topmost, the supreme expression of His glory. The Hebrew word for glory means weighty in splendor and heavy in greatness. The coming of Jesus to this earth represented the splendor and greatness of God in the highest way possible.

This perception of Christmas can elevate all we do to commemorate this time of year. Celebrating Christmas and everything it truly represents is to sing with the angels "Glory to God in the highest." The Bible says it just does not get any better than that!

"Blessed is the King who comes in the name of the Lord! Peace in heaven and glory in the highest." (Luke 19:38 NKJV)

Individual Activity: Think about noble causes espoused by the world. Decide in your heart how they compare to God's cause, which is the eternal salvation of mankind.

Family Activity: Discuss some important historical events that have happened in the world. Your list might include the end of a war, or the discovery of a new medicine, or the invention of computers. As wonderful as these incidents may be, God says the greatest event in all of mankind's history is when Jesus came to earth.

YOUR REFLECTIONS

DECEMBER

21

IN THE ABSENCE OF CHRISTMAS CHEER

Follow the Light to Hope

Christmas is known for creating warm, fuzzy feelings for many people. Some of us seem to be more cheerful and joyful during the holiday season. For those whose families and friends are close, and troubles seem so far away, a happy Christmas is easily attained. However, what happens when you are lonely, or depressed, or grieving, or sick, or facing seemingly insurmountable difficulties? A merry Christmas may seem as likely to happen as a snowstorm in Death Valley.

As much as we would like to "rise above it all," our circumstances greatly influence our ability to find joy in Christmas. Expectations of Christmas perfection sets us up for more sadness than gladness. When we are bombarded with images of the ideal Christmas, we find that the difficulties of our own reality are magnified. For some "wake me up when it is over" sounds like the best way to cope.

If you have ever felt this way, you are in good company. The first Christmas was not Hallmark movie material. Pregnant Mary suffered physically on the back of a donkey during a ninety-mile trek in her last trimester. She gave birth separated from her family and closest friends. During this time in history, childbirth was painful and risky business. Joseph was dealing with the stress of homelessness and the pressure of being responsible for the well-being of the Son of God! Fear, pain, separation, anxiety. The struggle was real. There were no visions of sugar plums dancing in their heads on this night. The circumstances were daunting to say the least, yet ....

The angels' good tidings produced not just joy, but great joy. The promise of the Savior overshadowed the troubles of this world and all who heard it rejoiced. Mary's and Joseph's circumstances did not change, but their perspectives did. The angel bore a heavenly message and "the things of earth grow strangely dim in the light of His glory and grace."

Amidst the fear, pain and struggle, there is hope. "For unto you is born this day a Savior." Even in the absence of Christmas cheer, you can still celebrate the hope of promised grace. For those who trust in Him, there is a better day coming.

"May our Lord Jesus Christ himself and God our Father, who loved us and by his grace gave us eternal encouragement and good hope, encourage your heart and strengthen you in every good deed and word." (2 Thessalonians 2:16 NIV)

Individual Activity: If there is sadness in your heart this Christmas season, contemplate the words of 2 Thessalonians 2:16 and allow it to begin to affect your perspective.

Family Activity: Talk about a sad event in the past. Then discuss a happy occasion everyone is looking forward to. This is a reminder of God's promise that sadness does not last forever for his children.

YOUR REFLECTIONS

DECEMBER

22

THE PEACE OF CHRISTMAS

Follow the Light to Reconciliation

In 1914, on the frontlines of World War I, there occurred a spontaneous, unprecedented, and never-repeated incident. On Christmas Eve, in trenches only yards apart, British, French, and German soldiers began to sing Christmas carols. Soon the soldiers started to emerge from their foxholes and came together in "no man's land." In the absence of the shelling and the shooting, they shared food, souvenirs, and stories of their loved ones at home. They even respectfully buried their dead. In this rare moment in time, there was a fleeting and temporary peace.

Almost two thousand years before this event, the Christmas angels also sang a song of peace, "Peace on earth; good will toward men." They were messengers sent from heaven to announce an everlasting peace being offered to the people of earth.

Unlike the 1914 Christmas truce, which was simply the temporary absence of conflict between two groups of people, the heavenly message refers to an everlasting peace between God and anyone who would receive His truth. One of the primary definitions of the Greek word for peace is reconciliation. Reconciliation of a sinful people to a holy God is the purpose of the God-Man born on Christmas day. The angels' song can be paraphrased, "Reconciliation (peace) has come to earth, due to God's kindness (goodwill) directed toward mankind."

"For He Himself is our peace ...." (Ephesians 2:14 NKJV)

The peace of Christmas is a not a treaty or a state of mind, it is a person, and His name is Jesus."

"For it pleased the Father that in Him all the fullness should dwell; and by Him to reconcile all things to Himself, by Him, whether things on earth or things in heaven, having made peace through the blood of His cross." (Colossian1:19, 20 NKJV)

Individual Activity: Recall a time in your life when a relationship was broken. You may or may not have been able to repair it. Remember, only Jesus can reconcile a broken relationship with God, which can help heal relationships on earth.

Family Activity: Talk about a time when someone in your family had an argument and used angry words. Did someone intervene and make peace? Since we all do things that make God unhappy, Jesus came to make peace with God for us as only He can.

YOUR REFLECTIONS

DECEMBER

23

THE FIRST MISSIONARIES

Follow the Light to Salvation

They lived their lives with few, if any, human amenities. The shepherds were isolated and unclean as they dwelled among their sheep. Even sleep was a luxury as they watched over their flock through the night.

However, the events they experienced this night changed everything. A messenger from God bathed in unapproachable light appeared. Knowing they were in the presence of holiness caused them to be greatly afraid. However, the angel bore good tidings of great joy. A Savior was born.

When the angel went back to heaven and the shepherds began to regain their senses, their first desire was to find the Savior. They hurried to Bethlehem to see this thing that had come to pass. When they found the Christ child and accepted in their hearts that all the angel had said was true, they shared the good news with anyone who would listen. Their lives became filled with glorifying and praising God.

What a beautiful picture of salvation the lowly shepherds provide for us as we watch them become followers of Christ! In the fields that night, they came face to face with the knowledge that they were unclean and unworthy to be in the presence of the holy God. Their great fear was soon replaced with hope as the news of the Savior was revealed. This ignited a desire to seek Him. They sought Him, they found Him, and they believed in Him. He transformed their lives, and they could not keep this wonderful reality to themselves. So, they became the first missionaries of the gospel of Jesus Christ.

May our salvation cause us to rejoice this Christmas with the same enthusiasm as the shepherds, because Christmas really is Good News.

"For by grace, you have been saved through faith, and that not of yourselves; it is the gift of God, not of works, lest anyone should boast." (Ephesians 2:8-9 NKJV)

Individual Activity: Have you sought, found, and trusted in Jesus? If so, follow the example of the shepherds, and share the Good News with others.

Family Activity: Remember a time you received some good news. Maybe you found out a baby was on the way, or you won a ballgame, or you were going on a fun trip. Did you get excited? Did you want to tell someone your good news? The shepherds felt the same way. They had the best news in the world and could not wait to tell everyone who would listen.

YOUR REFLECTIONS

DECEMBER

24

A RELATIONSHIP WITH CHRISTMAS

Follow the Light to Christ

Family Christmas gatherings are a huge part of my Christmas memories. I am using the word huge literally. Both of my parents came from large families. So, we attended two family Christmas parties every year, which meant that I celebrated Christmas with over fifty relatives annually. It was chaotic and crowded, but we never ran low on food or fun.

Even though my grandparents' homes were crammed with relatives, it does not mean I had close relationships with everyone in the houses. Some of them I only saw once or twice a year; others were a significant part of my life. I had many relatives and only a few relationships.

The meaning of the original Greek word for relationship means "someone who remains close alongside." We know from the creation story in Genesis that God created people to be relational. It is in our DNA to thrive in close, loving relationships. It is this attribute that allows God to draw us to Himself. It is the reason Jesus was born of woman and became like us. He desires a relationship with us.

Without a relationship with Christ, Christmas has no lasting meaning. It is little more than a momentary flash of warm feelings, much like the light of a falling star. The significance of Christmas is found in the bond we have with Jesus. The celebrating of Christmas is meant to help us focus on "remaining close alongside" our Savior. As you enjoy the festivities of the season, remember to pray that all may have a personal relationship with the Christ in Christmas.

We have seen for ourselves and continue to state openly that the Father sent His Son as Savior of the world. Everyone who confesses that Jesus is God's Son participates continuously in an intimate relationship with God. We know it so well, we have embraced it heart and soul, this love that comes from God. (1 John 4:14-16 The Message)

Individual Activity: Embrace the loving relationship God offers you. Immerse yourself in Christ's love for you. It will impact all other relationships in your life.

Family Activity: Look at some family photos of people with whom you have close relationships (someone who remains close alongside). Pray that they will have a merry Christmas. Then call them and say I love you.

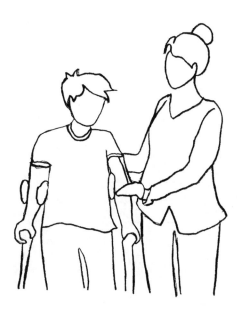

YOUR REFLECTIONS

DECEMBER
25

SET APART

Follow the Light to the Holy One

At Christmastime, there is a danger of settling for the thrill of opening presents and the jolly camaraderie of friends and family. However, Christmas is more than our commercialized culture would have us believe. Unfortunately, we can easily miss the quiet joy of realizing there is something greater than ourselves to celebrate. You will only experience the deeper meaning of Christmas if you deliberately set aside time to seek it. When you do, you will find the Holiness that resides in the true celebration of the season.

To be holy is to be set apart for a special purpose, as was the Christ child. From the moment of His conception, He was unique and set apart to accomplish the salvation of all people for all time. He became the unblemished Lamb of God who would take away the sins of the world.

If your heart has followed the Light this Christmas season, your journey will end today in the presence of the Holy One. Connect your holiday traditions to the Savior and they too will be set apart for His purposes. It is His holiness that can penetrate our Christmas and elevate it to a season set apart for the sacred and not just the secular.

So, in addition to a merry Christmas this year, I also wish you and your family a Holy Christmas always.

"And the angel answered and said to her, 'The Holy Spirit will come upon you, and the power of the Highest will overshadow you; therefore, also, that Holy One who is to be born will be called the Son of God.'" (Luke 1:35 NKJV)

Individual Activity: Find a quiet place and time to read the Christmas story from the Bible. (Luke 2:1-20 and Matthew 2:1-11)

Family Activity: Gather the family around and read the Christmas story from the Bible. (Luke 2:1-20 and Matthew 2:1-11)

YOUR REFLECTIONS

THE CHRISTMAS STORY
LUKE 2:1-20 TLB

About this time, Caesar Augustus, the Roman emperor, decreed that a census should be taken throughout the nation. (This census was taken when Quirinius was governor of Syria.)

Everyone was required to return to his ancestral home for this registration. And because Joseph was a member of the royal line, he had to go to Bethlehem in Judea, King David's ancient home, journeying there from the Galilean village of Nazareth. He took with him Mary, his fiancée, who was obviously pregnant by this time. And while they were there, the time came for her baby to be born, and she gave birth to her first child, a son. She wrapped him in a blanket and laid him in a manger, because there was no room for them in the village inn.

That night some shepherds were in the fields outside the village, guarding their flocks of sheep. Suddenly an angel appeared among them, and the landscape shone bright with the glory of the Lord. They were badly frightened, but the angel reassured them.

"Don't be afraid!" he said. "I bring you the most joyful news ever announced, and it is for everyone! The Savior—yes, the Messiah, the Lord—has been born tonight in Bethlehem! How will you recognize him? You will find a baby wrapped in a blanket, lying in a manger!"

Suddenly, the angel was joined by a vast host of others—the armies of heaven—praising God: "Glory to God in the highest heaven," they sang, "and peace on earth for all those pleasing him."

When this great army of angels had returned again to heaven, the shepherds said to each other, "Come on! Let's go to Bethlehem! Let's see this wonderful thing that has happened, which the Lord has told us about."

They ran to the village and found their way to Mary and Joseph. And there was the baby, lying in the manger. The shepherds told everyone what had happened and what the angel had said to them about this child. All who heard the shepherds' story expressed astonishment, but Mary quietly treasured these things in her heart and often thought about them.

Then the shepherds went back again to their fields and flocks, praising God for the visit of the angels, and because they had seen the child, just as the angel had told them.

THE CHRISTMAS STORY
MATTHEW 2:1-12 TLB

Jesus was born in the town of Bethlehem, in Judea, during the reign of King Herod.

At about that time some astrologers from eastern lands arrived in Jerusalem, asking, "Where is the newborn King of the Jews? for we have seen his star in far-off eastern lands and have come to worship him."

King Herod was deeply disturbed by their question, and all Jerusalem was filled with rumors. He called a meeting of the Jewish religious leaders. "Did the prophets tell us where the Messiah would be born?" he asked. "Yes, in Bethlehem," they said, "for this is what the prophet Micah wrote: "O little town of Bethlehem, you are not just an unimportant Judean village, for a Governor shall rise from you to rule my people Israel."

Then Herod sent a private message to the astrologers, asking them to come to see him. At this meeting he found out from them the exact time when they first saw the star. Then he told them, "Go to Bethlehem and search for the child. And when you find him, come back and tell me so that I can go and worship him too!"

After this interview the astrologers started out again. And look! The star appeared to them again, standing over Bethlehem. Their joy knew no bounds!

Entering the house where the baby and Mary, his mother, were, they threw themselves down before him, worshiping. Then they opened their presents and gave him gold, frankincense, and myrrh. But when they returned to their own land, they didn't go through Jerusalem to report to Herod, for God had warned them in a dream to go home another way.

MAY YOUR LEGACY BE
A LIGHT TO FOLLOW

One of the greatest privileges in this life is the opportunity to influence the next generation for Christ. When you do, you produce lasting changes in eternity. No other legacy is more significant or more loving because this inheritance is not meant to leave something *for* someone; it is intended to leave something *in* someone.

May the following ten suggestions enhance your effort to make your legacy a light to be followed.

"He planted a witness in Jacob, set his Word firmly in Israel, then commanded our parents to teach it to their children, so the next generation would know, and all the generations to come will know the truth and tell the stories, so their children can trust in God." (Psalm 78:5-7 The Message)

Suggestion #1
LISTEN AND LEARN

A legacy is best received in the context of trust. One way to earn someone's trust is to give them your undivided attention. Listening intently to someone sounds easy, but it is not. Busy, distracted lives have become the norm, so giving someone your undivided attention no longer feels natural.

However, it is worth the self-discipline it takes to fully concentrate on another person. Undivided attention conveys respect and caring in a profound way. When we are willing to be truly interested in someone, we are placing value on them and their words.

Amazingly, when we listen, we learn what is in their heart. We have earned their trust and, only then, will they receive the spiritual legacy we have to share.

Anecdote: I have the wonderful opportunity to regularly enjoy the company of friends I knew in high school. One of the most meaningful parts of belonging to this small group is their willingness to listen well. Whenever I have trusted them with a need or a joy, everyone has given me the gift of undivided attention. It is a significant gift that opens the door of my heart.

Prepare to share by giving God's Word our close attention.

"We have seen and proved that what the prophets said came true. You will do well to pay *close attention* to everything they have written, for, like lights shining in dark corners, their words help us to understand many things that otherwise would be dark and difficult. But when you consider the wonderful truth of the prophets' words, then the light will dawn in your souls and Christ the Morning Star will shine in your hearts" (2 Peter 1:19 TLB)

Suggestion #2
TALK AND TEACH

Many teachable moments happen spontaneously. They are like fireflies. They flash unexpectedly and are gone in an instant. If you are not looking carefully, you can easily miss them. We need to maintain a heightened awareness of these momentary opportunities to share the truths, values, and virtues that we wish to pass on to the next generation.

Some teachable moments are like stars. These experiences are planned and intentional. We know when and where to look for them. Prayer before bedtime and meals, daily devotions, participating in church, and holiday traditions are examples of specific times set aside to talk about and teach the things of God.

Teachable moments fill our days. Taking advantage of them requires an awareness of the possibilities and a desire to leave a spiritual inheritance.

Anecdote: Once upon a time our family went fishing in the marshes of Saint Simon's Island. Everyone caught a variety of fish except me. I caught an eel, which the boat captain immediately asked if I wanted to hold. Everyone on board knew about my fear of anything remotely resembling a snake and assumed I would say no. However, I seized the teachable moment by ignoring my fear, holding the wiggly eel, and explaining to everyone it is possible to overcome being afraid. God did not give us a spirit of fear.

Prepare to share by embracing those moments when God's Word is teaching us.

"The whole Bible was given to us by inspiration from God and is useful to **teach** us what is true and to make us realize what is wrong in our lives; it straightens us out and helps us do what is right." (2 Timothy 3:16 TLB)

Suggestion #3
MAJOR ON THE MAJOR

It is tempting to allow things of lesser importance to consume the focus of our lives. We are susceptible to spending an inordinate amount of time in the pursuit of the temporary at the exclusion of the eternal. This quest can create a rat race that leaves little time for the more important aspects of living.

Time is the great equalizer. Every person on earth has twenty-four hours a day. How you allocate your time unerringly indicates what you value. Each day what you think about, what you do, and why you do it will consume your time and can set the mold for your future.

Whatever we allow to consume our time will create the strongest memories for the people in our lives. Each of us can purposely organize our priorities to make our relationships with God and others our primary concern. When we "major on the major." it will have a positive impact on what we pass on to those who come after us.

Anecdote: Years ago, I knew of a person who was continually treated for digestive problems. After wasting precious months on treatments that didn't help, she had a colonoscopy. The diagnosis was advanced cancer. Sad things can happen when we major on the minor and ignore the significant.

Prepare to share by recognizing that the most important thing to God should be the most important thing to us.

"Oh, Timothy, don't fail to do these things that God entrusted to you. Keep out of foolish arguments with those who boast of their 'knowledge' and thus prove their lack of it. Some of these people have missed the **most important thing in life**—they don't know God. May God's mercy be upon you." (1 Timothy 6:20-21 TLB

Suggestion #4
IT'S NOT ABOUT YOU

On the first page of the first chapter of Rick Warren's book *A Purpose Driven Life*, you will find this statement "It is not about you." This is a simple, but profound truth that will impact our legacy. When we consider being a good influence on others, we must start here.

As we relate with people around us, it is tempting to want to interact in ways that make us happy, even if it is not necessarily the wisest choice for the other person. When we consider what we leave behind, it will mean the most when we desire the best for the people we love.

Anecdote: As grandparents, who love nothing more than the laughter and joy of our grandchildren, this suggestion is a struggle. We must constantly remind ourselves that giving them cookies, candy, and coke every time they ask is not teaching healthy choices. Even though buying them something every time we go to the Dollar Store will get us a big hug, it will soon spoil them. We need to be reminded that it is not about us!

Prepare to share by humbling ourselves.

"And now this word to all of you: You should be like one big happy family, full of sympathy toward each other, loving one another with tender hearts and **humble minds**." (1 Peter 3:8 TLB)

Suggestion #5
BE GENUINE

Do as I say and not as I do. This is not the attitude that will build a healthy legacy. People tend to remember the hypocrisy rather than the truth you want them to emulate. Since none of us are perfect, being genuine is a goal we must strive to attain.

The most effective way you can influence another person to assimilate the values, virtues, and truths you hope to pass down is to model them. When Jesus embraced humanity and lived a sinless life, He gave us a perfect, genuine example of how we should live. He alone was able to live a guileless life.

Anecdote: To be perfectly genuine all the time is beyond me. It is not a trait that is inherent in my nature. When I do a good deed, I am more like an onion with layers that need to be peeled off. The first and most shallow motive is usually the desire to be liked or to impress someone. (I ask forgiveness for this one.) The second layer is the motivation to help another person. (Good, but not the best.) The third layer is the desire to bring glory to God. (Finally, a genuine heart.)

Prepare to share by examining our motives.

"What I am eager for is that all the Christians there will be filled with love that comes from *pure hearts*, and that their minds will be clean and their faith strong." (1 Timothy 1:5 TLB)

Suggestion #6
NOW IS THE TIME

The word "now" creates a sense of urgency. "I need this done now." "We must leave now." "You need to stop that right now." This urgency comes from the fact that now is the only time when we can act. We can remember the past and look forward to the future, but we live in the present.

Building on the legacies left by the people who have gone before us, we create our legacy now. The truths you want instilled in the hearts of the people you love need to be taught now. The values and virtues you desire to build into their character must be modeled today.

You cannot change the past and you cannot control the future, but you can act today and every day to construct the spiritual inheritance you want to leave behind. You are never too young or too old to start legacy building.

Anecdote: This book was originally written for my children and grandchildren. I procrastinated and was intimidated by the task of publishing a book. I almost talked myself out of going through the whole process. However, as I grow older, the urgency of "now" becomes stronger every day; therefore, Follow the Light to Christmas has become a reality.

Prepare to share by taking action today.

"But **now is the time**. Never forget the warning, "Today if you hear God's voice speaking to you, do not harden your hearts against him …." (Hebrews 3:15 TLB)

Suggestion #7

BE INTENTIONAL

Take stock of the character attributes that are important to you. Does your list include the traits listed in the Bible: love, joy, peace, patience, kindness, goodness, gentleness, faithfulness, and self-control? This list is just a start. There are probably many more virtues you espouse.

You need to be aware of the characteristics you desire to be replicated in the lives of the people you influence. Knowing the desired outcome is the only way you can be intentional about what you share.

Write a list of your valued character traits. Make plans that model these traits. Use teachable moments to talk about the traits. Be intentional and build a legacy of faith and strong character.

Anecdote: My husband's father fought in World War II. In the army over three years, he fought in four campaigns including D Day. On Memorial Day, we intentionally talk about Granddaddy's courage. We plan to take our family to a military cemetery one day to impress upon them the courage of many people who fought for our country.

Prepare to share by living purposefully.

"As the time drew near for his return to heaven, he moved steadily onward toward Jerusalem with an **iron will**." (Luke 9:15 TLB)

Suggestion #8
PRAY

Prayer is required to accomplish anything of everlasting significance. None of the other suggestions listed here have any lasting power without prayer. A spiritual legacy undergirded with prayer releases the Holy Spirit to work in our lives and the hearts of those for whom we pray.

We have no control over the world in which generations to come will live. However, our prayers and actions now will be part of God's plan to prepare them for whatever they may face in the future.

Anecdote: This woman was born twenty-fifth in a family of twenty-five children. She gave birth to nineteen children with only ten living beyond infancy. Her name was Susanna Wesley. Struggling in a difficult marriage, raising the children was primarily Susanna's responsibility.

How did she do it? One strategy she used was prayer. She would throw her apron over her head and pray. All the children knew what she was doing and were instructed not to interrupt their mother while she prayed. Did it work? It would appear so. Two of her offspring, John and Charles Wesley, are considered the founders of the Methodist denomination.

Prepare to share by praying daily for the spiritual future of your descendants.

"I am not praying for these alone but also for the *future believers* who will come to me because of the testimony of these." (John 17:20 TLB)

Suggestion #9
PRESERVE

It is wise to provide evidence of our legacy that lasts longer than we do. Coming generations will benefit from reminders of the truths we want them to retain. Be creative. Write letters, make videos, put together photo albums, keep a spiritual journal, create inspiring art, leave behind a Bible where you have marked significant passages, tell stories, record family experiences of faith on a flash drive, begin traditions, the list goes on and on. You might even want to write a book!

Anecdote: My mother-in-law spent most of her summers preserving food. Each summer her husband produced a bountiful garden, and the goal was that nothing would ever be wasted. She would labor into the night canning beans, freezing corn, drying apples, and shelling peas. Even so, they still had produce left to share with others. No one in her family ever went hungry.

Prepare to share by examining your faith and determining how you can pass it on.

"Now may the God of peace Himself sanctify you completely; and may your whole spirit, soul, and body be *preserved* blameless at the coming of our Lord Jesus Christ." (1 Thessalonians 5:23)

Suggestion #10

LOVE

As we contemplate these suggestions on ways to build a legacy, the last and most important aspect is our fundamental motivation. It must be love. Otherwise, our effort will be like sounding brass and a clanging cymbal. There is no place for pride and self-centeredness as we look to the future and those who will come after us. The goal is not to create a memorial to ourselves, but rather a light that will lead to Jesus, because loving Jesus is the greatest legacy of all.

"Three things will last forever faith, hope, and love, and the *greatest of these is love.*" (1 Corinthians 13:13 NLT)

MY JOURNEY TO THE LIGHT

He was there for me on the day I was born; of course, I was oblivious to His presence. However, at a very early age, He was introduced to my young self. I was singing songs and listening to stories about Jesus as a preschooler in a little clapboard church. During my childhood years, He was a comfortable and reassuring presence for me, even though I did not actually know Him personally yet.

"When I was a child, I spoke as a child, I understood as a child." (1 Corinthians 13:11 KJV)

As a preteen, I began to recognize how important He was and how much I needed Him to protect me from immense danger in the future. For the first time, at the age of twelve, in childlike faith, I opened my heart and turned to Him and the security He provided. After making that decision at a spring revival church service, I was baptized in a river near the church. However, the peaceful assurance that all was well did not last through the next phase of my life.

The tumult so often experienced in the teenage years impacted my relationship with Him. Concerns about my ability to trust and surrender caused doubts to arise, and so began the anxiety that would haunt me for the next fifteen years. These disturbing doubts were ignited by a poem I read as a sophomore in my high school literature class. In this poem, the author expressed a fatalistic view of death that I had never considered before; the foreboding idea that after you die, you cease to exist. But life was busy, and I figured I had a long time to live, so I continuously made great efforts to relegate these thoughts to the far corners of my mind as much as possible.

As I moved into my twenties, the issues with my inability to accomplish my perceived part of the "salvation process" morphed into wondering about the very existence of God. This was never displayed in a rebellious attitude that sought in any way to defy God. It was an uneasiness and sense of foreboding that lingered in the back of my mind causing true peace to elude me. All this inward uncertainty co-existed with regularly attending church, teaching Sunday School, and singing in the choir.

If this was not enough trouble, it was also a time of considerable self-centeredness. I hid it well; but so many things I did were based on what I wanted and thought I needed. Much to my chagrin, impressing others was much too important to me. Purity of motive was a real issue. Living a life that would bring honor to me was on my mind more than bringing honor to God.

As I was leaving the tumultuous twenties and entering my thirties, life changed, and so did I. Something happened that turned my world around. My children were born, and I truly began to understand that it was no longer about me. Sleepless nights, confinement, and constant attention—even though difficult parts of parenthood—were not considered sacrifices when it meant their needs were met. God had so many lessons in store for me through motherhood: unconditional love, the value of life, the joy of sacrificial giving, and the humble dependency of a young child. He would use these intensely personal truths to bring me to a change of heart and to Himself in a relationship of peace, trust, and surrender.

When I was thirty-two years old and pregnant with my daughter, my invisible struggle came to a head. After years of being active in the church and sincerely seeking answers, I gave up. I felt like a marathon runner who had taken her last step and crumpled into a heap of mental and spiritual exhaustion.

One evening I was working in the kitchen and I began to weep. I told God I could not carry the crushing weight of doubt any longer. I had tried to get all the steps right: repent, trust, obey. It had been drilled into me that those were my responsibilities for salvation. In fact, I completed all three steps several times in my spiritual journey, but I could never *stay* repented or *stay* trusting or *stay* obedient and every time I faltered, in my mind, my salvation was at risk. This resulted in no peace and no security ever. I finally threw in the towel figuratively speaking. The idea that I had any ability to make and keep myself right with God was obliterated. I was as helpless as a newborn infant. I prayed either it is all you Jesus, or I have nothing.

Then I began to sing an old hymn that "popped" into my mind. "My hope is built on nothing less than Jesus' blood and righteousness; I dare not trust the sweetest frame; but wholly lean on Jesus' name. On Christ the solid rock I stand. All other ground is sinking sand." After having realized my need for a "solid rock," I became completely dependent on Jesus and His promises. This shift in my relationship with Him gave me the peace and security I had been pursuing for so long. I felt just like a child caught in a dangerous undertow whose only hope was to cling to the lifeguard who came to save her.

I wish I could say at that point I became a paragon of faith, but I did not. I still had some battles to fight, especially with fear and anxiety. The Lord used my husband's steadfastness and constancy as anchors that kept me from being swept away to dark places. Even so, I can say I have not wavered from the decision to believe there is a God, and He loved me enough to send His Son to die for me, and "my hope is built on nothing less."

With this firm foundation in place, most of my third decade was spent raising our children. I was unaware of how God was using this precious season of life to prepare me for a surprising and very unexpected journey with Him.

During my forty-fourth summer, my son was becoming a high school sophomore and my daughter was entering middle school. As a full-time homemaker, my responsibilities were shifting, and a quiet restlessness began to stir in me. Was there more to serving Jesus than being a faithful church member? Seeking the answer to this question led me and my husband to a life we could never have imagined.

When I understood the affirmative answer to the first question, it led me to a second. What did I have to offer? What service to Christ would give me the passion I needed to take this step of faith? The answer was my family. It was as plain as the nose on my face. I sincerely desired that every mother could have the opportunity to experience the blessing of her child as I had experienced the blessing of my children. This deeply held value led me to a pregnancy center where I learned to serve the Lord with my whole heart.

In August of 1999, I entered the Gwinnett Crisis Center (later to be known as the Pregnancy Resource Center of Gwinnett) as a completely unprepared volunteer. With a minimal amount of training, I soon found myself in a counseling room with a young woman struggling with an unplanned pregnancy, the first of many to follow in the next eighteen years. In the center, I witnessed everything from a college freshman who was so afraid of being pregnant that she swore she would never "do it" again to a disturbed young woman who was thirty-two weeks into her pregnancy and swore she did not even know she was pregnant. From a very inexperienced trainee, to a client services manager, to the center director, to the founding director of a statewide pregnancy center organization, I always felt as if I was in over my head, because I was. I worked on a continual learning curve and am absolutely convinced that I was dependent on the Lord to get me through the challenges that came with each position.

Upon retiring in March of 2017, I reflected on my pregnancy center life and realized how much the Lord had changed me. I remembered those lessons He had shown me in my parenting years about unconditional love, the value of life, the joy of sacrificial giving, and humble dependency on Him. These values had been the cornerstone of the work He had called me to do, and He had ingrained them into the person He had wanted me to become.

As I approached sixty years of age, God began to unleash His showers of sheer blessing. Grandchildren began to be born. For someone like me, the experience of your children having children goes beyond joy. The opportunity of being an integral part of their lives is the culmination of all He has sought to teach me. There is no greater mission in my life than to be part of the influence that leads them to Jesus.

In this season of my life, the question begins to change from "Where am I going?" to "What am I leaving behind?" What will last longer than wealth, fame, comfort, or anything this world has to offer? Even though I fail miserably (a lot), I yearn for my legacy to be love, joy, peace, patience, gentleness, kindness, goodness, faithfulness, and self-control. These are the things that are most like Jesus and Jesus will last forever.

I can see the thread of His abiding presence throughout my life. It was there in my beginning, has never left me, and will be there at my end. Therein lies my hope; and, someday, it is this hope I will leave to the generation to come.

EPILOGUE

This book was written to inspire all of us to recognize and reflect the glory of God. I humbly admit, it is not a sermon prepared by someone who has attained the goals presented. Every word represents lessons I am learning daily. Every perspective shared came through the filter of my need to know and understand God's direction. Every truth had to resonate in my heart before I could begin to write it.

"Not that I have already attained, or am already perfected; but I press on, that I may lay hold of that for which Christ Jesus has also laid hold of me." (Philippians 3:12 NKJV)

Perhaps your heart has been stirred to begin the journey of building your legacy. It would be an honor if part of that journey included sharing copies of *Follow the Light to Christmas*. If you would like to purchase a copy or copies, please go to: www.donnamperryauthor.com

Printed in the United States
by Baker & Taylor Publisher Services